MUSHROOM HUNTING

CHRONICLE BOOKS

SAN FRANCISCO

POCKET NATURE SERIES

Text copyright © 2023 by **EMILY HAN AND GREGORY HAN**.

Library of Congress Cataloging-in-Publication Data available.

ISBN 978-1-7972-2134-2

Manufactured in China.

MIX
Paper | Supporting responsible forestry
FSC™ C136333

Series concept and editing by **CLAIRE GILHULY**.
Series design by **LIZZIE VAUGHAN**.
Cover art by **LUCIA CALFAPIETRA**.
Interior illustrations by **LIANA JEGERS**.

Typeset in Albra, Benton Sans, Caslon.

Guinness World Records is a registered trademark of Guinness World Records Limited; Q-tips is a registered trademark of Conopco, Inc.; Super Mario Bros. is a registered trademark of Nintendo of America Inc.; Where's Waldo? is a registered trademark of DreamWorks Distribution Limited.

10 9 8 7 6 5 4 3 2

Chronicle books and gifts are available at special quantity discounts to corporations, professional associations, literacy programs, and other organizations. For details and discount information, please contact our premiums department at corporatesales@chroniclebooks.com or at 1-800-759-0190.

Chronicle Books LLC
680 Second Street
San Francisco, California 94107
www.chroniclebooks.com

CONTENTS

SPRING has come again.
And the EARTH
is like a child who
knows POEMS by heart.

—**Rainer Maria Rilke,** *Sonnets to Orpheus*
(translated by Willis Barnstone)

INTRODUCTION

Over a decade ago, an uncommonly wet season descended upon Southern California. The rains were noteworthy for both their early autumn arrival and the torrent they unleashed across the coastline, mountains, and foothills, reaching even into the distant desert. Parched and cracked from years of drought, the arid desert soil hid an enormous cache of seeds slumbering belowground, biding the return of more favorable conditions.

That rainy season would more than suffice. Months later, a kaleidoscopic explosion of wildflowers blanketed the Antelope Valley and Mojave Desert, drawing tens of thousands of visitors to revel in their huge swaths of color.

To this day, many remember it as one of the best wildflower seasons in recorded history.

But fewer people were aware of a similar and even rarer emergence across the landscape that same year. Revealing themselves mere days and weeks after the rainstorms, mushrooms—all different kinds—rose from the earth in a phenomenon that lasted well into spring.

For those attuned to the world of mushrooms, the appearance of rain promises a similar revival to mushrooms as it does flowers and plants. And like plants, fungi invest in the future too, dispersing vast quantities of spores into the air. Riding on the slightest hint of a breeze, a bird's wing, or the soles of your shoes, these microscopic spores find refuge in the cragged bark of wizened oak trees, beneath the fallen-leaf quilt work of sycamores, along the muddy banks of seasonal creeks, and even in the shaded corners of our backyards. There, the spores wait out dry spells in silent dormancy. Quenched by rainfall, they spring to life, germinating into mycelial fibers and fruiting into a wondrous array of mushrooms.

The ubiquity of fungi goes largely unnoticed where the two of us live in Los Angeles (Tongva, Kizh, and Chumash land). Occasionally, however, when conditions are right, as they were during that wildly rainy season, their presence becomes visible. We had spotted and admired mushrooms along trails in years past, yet our attention was fleeting. However, during that remarkably wet year, we experienced a conversion of sorts. One muddied step at a time, we transformed from dutiful, destination-oriented hikers into inquisitively slow-paced mushroom hunters.

Every walk or hike that year revealed life-forms previously unnoticed: mushrooms with spirited, coral-shaped "arms"; wildly maned fungi with white stalactites in lieu of gills; innumerable LBMs (little brown mushrooms, as they're colloquially called even among well-versed mycologists) carpeting stretches of creeksides; tiny nest-shaped fungi holding clutches of spore-filled "eggs"; and most memorably, the yolk-hued ellipses emerging from darkly sodden soil that would reveal themselves to be choice edible mushrooms: California golden chanterelles. It seemed as if a hidden world had emerged from the earth, inviting us to deepen our awareness.

Since that particularly bountiful year, our perception of the world around, beneath, and above us has sharpened. Any place can offer an opportunity to awaken our senses, to become more conscious of not only *where* mushrooms are to be found but also *why* they thrive and fruit in some places but not others.

This book is not a scientific guide or a guide to foraging for consumption, and neither of us is a professional mycologist. However, we share our experience as seasoned enthusiasts and published authors on topics ranging from plant medicine to landscape architecture and terrestrial gastropods. Over the years, we have sought mushrooms near and far (both in our backyard and on faraway travels), attended mycology talks and events, and participated in online mushroom communities. Our interest is driven not by what we can consume nor even necessarily what we can categorize. Instead, we are two people inspired by the sheer joy of discovering something previously unknown to us.

As you peruse this guide, you'll become oriented to the practices of mindful mushroom hunting and the benefits this activity can bring to your life. You'll find out what a mushroom is (and isn't) and learn beginner-friendly tips for when, where, and how to hunt for mushrooms safely. To help get you started, we share profiles of fifteen major types of mushrooms found around the world.

With this book, we hope to offer the mushroom-curious a doorway to a realm inhabited by life-forms performing the mundane and the magical, growing both large and small, and expressed in a multitude of forms, many of which will undoubtedly compel the question, *What is that?!*

See that EVERYTHING is impermanent and without ETERNAL IDENTITY. See that although things are IMPERMANENT and without lasting identity, they are nonetheless WONDROUS.

—Thích Nhất Hạnh, *The Miracle of Mindfulness*
  (translated by Mobi Warren)

I.

MUSHROOMS AND MINDFULNESS

We'll never know exactly what our earliest ancestors thought when they happened upon their first mushroom. Perhaps their eyes widened as they inspected an unknown fungus growing at the base of a tree or fruiting from a branch. Their hominid brains must have buzzed with wonder while investigating that which appeared as neither plant nor animal. First, a tentative touch (maybe with a stick), followed by a suspicious sniff before the most courageous—or foolish—ventured a taste. Whether this encounter resulted in joy or regret, we can only guess.

What we do know is the lives of humans and mushrooms have long intertwined, with mushrooms offering us food, medicine, and spiritual value. Our senses have always helped us navigate this relationship. Remnants of art in North Africa as far back as 9000 BCE reveal our appreciation for mushrooms was worthy of inscribing in stone. An aura of fantasy, mystery, and even danger has surrounded their fantastic forms that can appear and disappear seemingly overnight. Their potential effects on the body, including altered perception and even death, only add to their curious reputation.

The allure of wild mushrooms is often connected with a desire to gather them for consumption. And no doubt, mushroom foraging can be an enjoyable pastime. However, we propose another way to hunt for mushrooms: allowing them to guide us in the experience of mindful interaction with the Earth.

Today, we live in the most technologically connected era in history, yet many of us feel a sense of disconnection—from each other and the world around us. Rushing from one thing to the next, distracted by social media, and tangled up in the fear of missing out, we often overlook the wonders right in front of us. What if we slowed down to appreciate the dapple of sunshine, the taste of wind, the trill of a bird's song? Research shows that spending time in green spaces reduces stress and anxiety, restoring our emotional and physical well-being. Yet we've forgotten how to immerse ourselves in these experiences.

Even folks who regularly spend time outdoors often miss out on the deeper story of where they are. Going on a walk or hike intent on a magnificent view, then snapping a quick photo and turning away is like going to an art museum and merely glancing at the Mona Lisa. Imagine how different the experience might be if you stopped to notice the individual brushstrokes, prioritizing observation rather than a checklist of destinations.

Mushroom hunting gives us a path to quiet the wandering thoughts and chatter in our minds by relaxing into bodily awareness.

By using our senses, we can pay attention to our surroundings and remain open to what we encounter: the moisture in the air, the scent of soil underfoot, the presence or absence of sunlight. In this state of openness, we are more apt to find mushrooms! Yet even when we don't, we experience time well spent. Dwelling in neither the past nor the future, we can be fully in the here and now.

This activity is not hurried. While searching for and observing mushrooms, a different sense of time unfurls, one that is slower and more in tune with the rhythms of the living world. Mushrooms often emerge from dead trees, rotten logs, and decomposing leaves, giving us an opportunity to witness the cycles of life, death, and continuation. In their ephemeral presence, we can recognize that everything changes, nothing is permanent.

REISHI HOT COCOA

MAKES 2 SERVINGS

---

2 Tbsp coarsely
chopped
dried reishi
mushrooms

2 Tbsp
unsweetened
cocoa powder

2 Tbsp sugar
(or sweetener
of your choice)

¼ tsp ground
cinnamon

Small pinch salt

1 in [2.5 cm]
piece vanilla bean,
split and scraped

1 cup [240 ml]
milk of your
choice

Once revered as a tonic for Chinese emperors, lingzhi, or reishi, mushrooms support the immune system and help the body adapt to stress. Dried, sliced reishi can be found at apothecaries or health food shops. As you make and sip this pleasantly bittersweet drink, be open to your senses. Give your attention to the sound of the liquid simmering, the scents and colors of the ingredients, and the feel of the warm cup in your hands. Savor the experience without rush.

TO MAKE THE TEA: In a small pot, combine the reishi and 1¼ cups [300 ml] water.

cont.

Cover and bring to a boil over high heat. Lower the heat to low and simmer for 45 minutes. Strain through a fine-mesh strainer, pressing to extract as much liquid as possible; discard the solids. (The tea can be stored tightly sealed for up to one day in the refrigerator.)

TO MAKE THE HOT COCOA: In a saucepan, combine the cocoa powder, sugar (or other sweetener, if using), cinnamon, salt, and vanilla. Pour a couple of tablespoons of reishi tea into the pan and whisk until smooth. Bring the mixture to a simmer over medium-low heat. Gradually add the rest of the reishi tea and the milk to the cocoa mixture, whisking constantly. When the mixture is heated through, remove from heat. Discard the vanilla bean and serve immediately.

To experience FUNGI
through multiple SENSES
is a way to INTIMATELY
know them.

—**Alison Pouliot**, "Intimate Strangers of the Subterrain"

II.

WHAT IS A MUSHROOM?

We all know what a mushroom looks like. They're commonly found sliced and baked on pizzas or swimming in bowls of ramen. They crop up overnight across well-irrigated lawns and silently greet hikers while peeking from forest edges. They appear as squat, shuffling video game characters or logos denoting a counter-culture lifestyle. But despite their ubiquity, many of us are barely aware of what mushrooms really are.

This is hardly a surprise, as there are over one hundred thousand known species of mushrooms currently identified across the globe, with many more named every year. In 2016 alone, 2,500 species were newly described. Only recently has the scientific community become more receptive to the vast knowledge of local species known by Indigenous cultures. Like a lone morel poking out from beneath a bed of pine needles, our understanding of the larger story of mushrooms is only beginning to emerge.

Here are a few things we do know. Mushrooms are neither plants nor animals. Rather, they are fungi, a wide-ranging group that encompasses not only mushrooms but also yeasts, rusts, smuts, molds, and mildews. (Thus, all mushrooms are fungi, but not all fungi are mushrooms.) The mushroom we see is just one part of the life cycle of a fungus.

Think of a mushroom like an apple. Just as a fruit helps continue the life cycle of a tree, a mushroom emerges from fungus as an act of reproduction. Except in the case of a mushroom, the "tree" and "branch" from which this fruiting body grows are concealed from view. The main body of a fungus consists of microscopic filaments (*hyphae*), which are bundled into a rootlike network (*mycelium*) buried within soil, wood, or other substrates. These hidden threads are minuscule individually but can be extensive. In Oregon, a honey fungus (*Armillaria ostoyae*) has been found to cover about 3.7 square miles [9.6 square km]! Considered the largest living organism on Earth, this ancient "Humongous Fungus" is approximately 8,650 years old.

And similar to how an apple contains seeds, a mushroom contains thousands, or even billions, of microscopic spores. Once discharged, the tiny spores may be carried away on wind currents or raindrops. Other spores may be dispersed by animals—from hungry flies to human hikers—to settle elsewhere. Depending on the environment, the spores will germinate and grow into new fungi.

For a fungus to sprout a mushroom, conditions must be just right—the perfect confluence of temperature, humidity, fresh air, and (sometimes) light. Often appearing and collapsing within weeks, days, or even hours, mushrooms embody the concept of impermanence. Catching sight of them requires mindful awareness (and good timing).

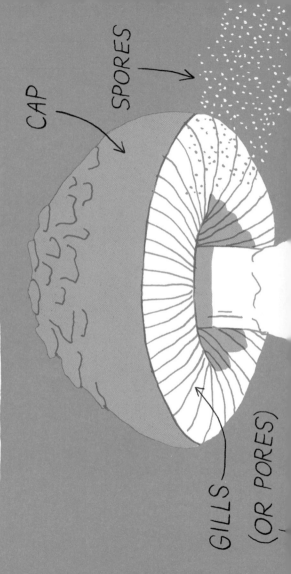

RING/SKIRT

STIPE/STEM

VOLVA

TUBES

(OR TEETH)

MYCELIAL THREADS (HYPHAE)

* NOT ALL MUSHROOMS HAVE ALL THESE PARTS

TYPES OF FUNGI

Unlike plants or animals, fungi do not photosynthesize or ingest their food. Rather, they absorb it from the world around them. They do this by growing into and around nutrient sources such as tree roots, wood chips, or even the body of a caterpillar.

Some fungi are *mycorrhizal*, which means they have intricate, mutualistic relationships with trees and shrubs. Beneath the soil's surface, these fungi's hyphae receive sugars and carbon from the plants' rootlets. In exchange, the fungi extend the surface area of the roots so the plants can absorb water and nutrients. Mycelia can even connect different plants' roots to each other. In the process, they help plants communicate chemical signals in a system commonly described as the wood wide web.

About 90 percent of land plants have mycorrhizal associations with fungi—a type of relationship that first emerged four to five hundred million years ago. Back then, plants stood only a few feet tall, while spires of fungi reached heights of up to 24 feet [7.3 meters]! Today, tree families that commonly have mycorrhizal relationships include *Fagaceae* (beech, oak), *Betulaceae* (birch, alder), *Salicaceae* (willow, poplar), and *Pinaceae* (fir, spruce, pine).

Another group of fungi, called *saprotrophic*, *saprophytic*, or *saprobic* fungi, are decomposers who feed on dead organic remains such as wood, fallen leaves, other fungi, or herbivore dung. They break down essential nutrients like carbon and nitrogen, returning them to the soil and water to be used again by plants and animals. Some saprotrophs are specialists, focusing on specific foods like pine needles or oak stumps. Consider them the Earth's greatest recyclers.

Other fungi have *parasitic* relationships and are predators or pathogens on living plants (on tree bark, for example), animals like ants or caterpillars, or even other mushrooms. But try not to think of these relationships in terms of "good" versus "bad." This does a dis-service to the vital role fungi play in recycling nutrients within an ecosystem.

One of the most surprising things you'll learn about fungi is that some have relationships with various insects. Certain leaf-cutting ants, mound-building termites, and ambrosia beetles are like farmers, cultivating fungi for food. In exchange, the fungi receive nutrients in the form of organic matter and help dispersing their spores. A win-win.

And then there are *lichens*. More than just a fungus, a lichen is a partnership between a fungus and an *alga* or bacterium that photosynthesizes. In these symbiotic relationships, the fungus provides most of the lichen's shape and fruit body, while absorbing water and nutrients from trees, soil, or even rocks. Meanwhile, the alga or cyanobacterium creates food through photosynthesis.

By creating partnerships and recycling nutrients, fungi promote the health of the world around them. In addition to the relationships we've described, fungi hold soil together, sequester carbon (thus reducing the amount in the atmosphere), and provide food for animals, including insects, gastropods, nematodes, birds, and mammals. And we haven't even touched upon the ever-growing list of wondrous things people are working with fungi for, from removing plastic pollution to being used as sustainable building material. Constantly surprising us with their adaptability, fungi are essential to the past, present, and future of life on Earth.

SLIME MOLD

Slime molds are another bizarre life-form you might want to look for. Slimy and often brightly colored, many resemble fungi in shape and in their preference for cool, moist conditions, such as in rotting logs and decaying leaves. Like fungi, slime molds play an important role in breaking down organic matter.

There is a way that NATURE SPEAKS, that land speaks. Most of the time we are simply not PATIENT enough, QUIET enough, to pay attention to the story, to be ATTENTIVE.

—**Linda Hogan,** in *Listening to the Land* by Derrick Jensen

III.

WHEN, WHERE, AND HOW
TO FIND MUSHROOMS

On certain still mornings, the dampened veil of evening lingers long enough to greet the earliest rays of golden warmth. We hear our own breath moving in unison with the squelch of sodden earth from our footfalls. In these moments, there seems a silent promise that mushrooms will be found by those who seek them. In Russian, this sort of premonition is called грибной дождь (gribnoy dozhd), or the "mushroom rain." Every mushroom enthusiast relies on subtle sensory cues. As you develop your mushroom hunting skills, you, too, will become attuned to why, when, and where fungi appear.

Most of us have hiked to a scenic destination to reach a breathtaking waterfall or ascend to a majestic vista. But how many of us stop to notice the details along the way? Mindful mushroom hunting doesn't lead to any single destination; rather, the "destination" is all around us. Though mushrooms are often associated with woodlands, fungi can also appear in grasslands, pastures, gardens, lawns, compost piles, riparian areas along streams and rivers, disturbed soils, and sandy coastal or desert areas—and even alongside potted plants. Wherever you search, mycelium and other life-forms are underfoot.

. . .

What you will find on your mushroom hunting journey depends not only on where you are but also on how you cultivate your senses. Even if you are hunting in your own backyard, try observing the world around you with the curious gaze of a child experiencing something new.

NOTES ON PICKING MUSHROOMS

Occasionally, you'll want to pick a mushroom to look at it more closely. Remember to keep the health of the fungi and their habitat in mind. Minimize disturbance and avoid overpicking, as animals may rely on them for food. (Also be aware of any local rules or laws.) Focus on mature mushrooms that have likely released many of their spores, helping to ensure their reproduction.

Depending on the mushroom, carefully pluck the fruit or cut it at the base, taking care not to damage the mycelium below. Cover up any hole left in the ground. Finally, help spread any remaining spores by placing the fruit body somewhere the wind can catch them, such as in the fork of a tree.

Practice scanning the environment. While you move (or stay in place), look for the presence of trees, like oaks or firs, which mycorrhizal mushrooms associate with, as well as leaf duff, fallen logs, and unusual shapes or flashes of color. *Mycophiles* (mushroom enthusiasts) often cast our eyes downward, searching for *shrumps*—humps in the soil pushed up by emerging mushrooms—or other fungal signs. If you can, crouch down to look for tiny mushrooms in damp grass or on the underside of a leaf. Also, don't forget to look up and all around! Some mushrooms appear overhead on weakened or diseased tree trunks and branches, requiring us to crane our necks upward to spy their presence. When you do find a mushroom, stop for a while. Say hello. Take in the details of the mushroom's shape or of the tiny snail feasting on its cap.

Searching for mushrooms isn't an act just of looking but also of feeling—for example, notice the sensation of humidity against your skin. Some mushrooms can thrive with just a little moisture in the leaf litter, maybe from fog or a light sprinkle, while others require heavy rains to soak into the ground. Become attuned to potential mushroom hunting opportunities, like after recent rains, snow-melts, or irrigation in a garden.

Because mushrooms require just the right temperature, humidity, and nutrition to grow, there is often a very limited window in which to find them. Most mushrooms prefer temperate weather. Once the air becomes too hot or cold, fungi are less likely to fruit. While this limits "mushroom season" to spring and autumn in many places, in certain climates they may fruit through summer or winter. However, you might notice these conditions shift as you move only a few feet to a different part of your yard or walking trail. Paying close attention to these subtle changes will increase your chances of finding mushrooms.

If you were a mushroom, what would you like to eat? Maybe an old tree stump, a pile of leaf litter, or a fallen pine cone. No one gets more excited about a rotten log than a mushroom hunter! Get in the habit of searching for saprobic mushrooms when you see or smell decaying leaves or wood. Sometimes, you might literally smell fungi itself. Follow your nose and see if you can figure out where the scent is coming from.

MUSHROOM HUNTING SAFETY

When mushroom hunting, it's important to be aware of your surroundings. In the excitement of finding mushrooms, it can be easy to overlook hazards like slippery surfaces, poisonous plants, or wildlife. (Our first few years of mushroom hunting were painfully punctuated by run-ins with poison oak.)

Very few mushrooms are deadly. Most poisonous mushrooms would just give you a bad stomach-ache if ingested. However, eating certain species can be fatal, so never forage and consume wild mushrooms unless you are experienced with iden-tification. The good news is that all mushrooms are safe to be around and even touch. The amount of toxin, if any, absorbed through your skin would be harmless. (Do wash your hands before grab-bing a snack, however.)

While you might want to avoid inhaling a large puff of spores (see page 89), there's no need to fear the air around mushrooms. Take a deep breath and enjoy your time outside!

Mushrooms aren't known for making a racket, but hearing can also be an important tool. Quieting chatter among hiking companions, limiting interruptions like app notifications, and leaving off headphones can help you better focus on the present moment and your surroundings. Can you detect the crunch of fallen leaves, the sound of water, or birds singing?

Realigning our senses isn't difficult, but it can take time. By slowing down and focusing on the details of your surroundings, your perceptions will deepen. One way to do this is to practice using one sense at a time. We all have unique sensory abilities and strengths, and there is no right or wrong approach. Perhaps you'll focus on your sense of smell for your whole walk. Or commit to spending just a minute feeling the air on your skin, then a minute noticing any shifts in your muscle tension, and so on.

While your body will be your best guide, also consider bringing tools such as a hand lens or macro lens (to look at small details like gills and pores); a camera; and a notebook or note-taking app. If you are going to be cutting mushrooms open to observe textures or colors, a pocketknife can be useful.

With each foray, the clues you find will help grow your knowledge. Look for mushrooms where you've seen them before; oftentimes they fruit year after year in the same place. Also pay attention to the conditions, such as weather, habitat, and substrate, in which you find certain types of mushrooms. In time, you may develop a sense of how to think like a mushroom, imagining the places where they prefer to grow.

Have patience, too. Sometimes you see a mushroom the moment you step on a trail, while other times it takes an hour to settle into an attentive state. Certain years may offer bumper crops, while other years may be lean. Sometimes you won't locate any mushrooms at all. No matter what you find, simply spending time outside, being present without hurry, and letting go of expectations is deeply worthwhile.

Turn over a ROCK,
dig under the ROOTS
of a tree, scoop up
a handful of WATER,
open your mouth:
THERE BE THE FUNGI.

—Doug Bierend, *In Search of Mycotopia*

IV.

MUSHROOMS TO LOOK FOR

The world of mushrooms presents an astonishing diversity of shapes, colors, textures, and fruiting habits. As many as four or five million fungi may exist globally, yet mycologists estimate more than 90 percent remain unclassified. While it would be impossible to create an encyclopedic guide to *all* the mushrooms you may encounter, we've compiled a list of "greatest hits" to spark your curiosity and jumpstart your search.

In this chapter, you'll find an overview of fifteen major types of mushrooms found across the world. These broad groups are based on typical mushroom forms rather than scientific classifications or genetic relationships. Characteristics vary with species or location, so we will focus on main features common to each mushroom type, along with some notable examples and mindful ways to interact with them.

When you find one of these mushrooms in the field, remember it isn't just a box to tick or a goal achieved. Think of the moment as an invitation to spend time with the mushroom. Stop, take a deep breath, check in with your senses, and notice how it feels to be in this time and place. The practice isn't merely a calming exercise (though you will probably feel a sense of tranquility). Many mushrooms fruit in the same spots year after year, around the same time, or under similar conditions. Taking note of these sensory cues can increase your odds of finding mushrooms in seasons to come.

If you are interested in further mushroom identification, we recommend checking out a field guide specific to your region. You can also learn how to make spore prints, as spore color is often key to identifying fungi. But there's no need to get caught up in identification at first (or ever)! Enjoying the process of discovering something new to you can be more than enough. But who knows? Your astute observations may lead you to become the first person to notice a mushroom new to science and lead to its formal identification (a mushroom hunter's dream).

WHAT'S IN A NAME?

If you're new to mushrooms or mostly interested in practicing mindfulness (rather than foraging to eat, for instance, which would require a different kind of guide), it is absolutely fine to simply enjoy them for who they are. Mushrooms can first and foremost be appreciated for their forms, colors, scents, and textures—and for the time you spend with them. There's no need to memorize names or worry about diving down the rabbit hole of taxonomic identification.

So why even learn a mushroom's name? Sometimes a mushroom's common name is helpful in identification ("those little mushrooms do look like bird's nests!"). A name may reveal shared or unique identifying characteristics (e.g., the blue-tinged blewit). Common names can also be quite evocative and memorable. Bleeding tooth, amethyst deceiver, dog stinkhorn, destroying angel, and the veiled lady are some of our favorites.

However, common names can vary regionally, and sometimes people use the same name for different species of mushrooms. Eventually, you may want to venture into learning scientific names, which eliminate ambiguity and offer access to a shared language for mycologists around the globe. Latin-based scientific names consist of two parts. For example, the shiitake mushroom, *Lentinula edodes*, belongs to the genus *Lentinula* and the species *edodes* within that genus. Mushrooms in the same genus (plural: genera) have shared characteristics. Knowing genus and species information can be helpful if you'd like to look up mushrooms in field guides or other resources.

A
MUSHROOM
FIELD GUIDE

GILLED MUSHROOMS

Close your eyes for a moment and imagine a mushroom—any mushroom. You might be envisioning a white stem topped with a cherry-red cap covered in white polka dots, with fine gills underneath its cap. There might even be a caterpillar lounging around as a companion. From early childhood on, *Amanita muscaria* (a.k.a. fly agaric) represents the quintessential fungus among us. It is mentioned in fairy tales and folklore and has been popularized by Super Mario Bros. It is the only mushroom deemed universally recognizable enough to earn its own emoji.

This photogenic fungus is one of a broad and varied group known as *gilled mushrooms*. While not always genetically related, all share the physical attributes of a cap-and-stem structure paired with gills. On the underside of the cap, the gills radiate like spokes from the mushroom's central stalk. These papery, bladelike structures are where the mushroom produces spores. Protected by the cap, the spores reside on the gills until they're ready to be carried off by the wind, disturbed by a passing animal, or even ingested and then dispersed in excrement. At the right time and with proper illumination, you can even witness spores flowing from the cap as sultry wisps.

Gilled mushrooms offer a diverse array of cap shapes, colors, and textures. Bell-shaped, conic, convex, knob-like, wavy-edged, brittle, rubbery, fuzzy, scaly, slimy, and warty are just a few of the shapes and textures you might encounter. Some are minuscule, practically pinheads only a couple of millimeters wide. Others grow up to nearly a foot [30 cm] broad. The members of one entire subcategory of gilled mushrooms are so abundant yet difficult to distinguish, they're popularly referred to as *LBMs*, or little brown mushrooms. Mushrooms in the *Russula* genus are much more distinct. Often large and vibrant, these mycorrhizal mushrooms provide food for deer, squirrels, and slugs; look for bite marks in the colorful caps.

Various species of gilled mushrooms are mycorrhizal, saprophytic, or parasitic. You may find them growing singly or in groups everywhere from the deepest forests to fairy rings in open fields. (Fairy rings are circles of mushrooms fruiting from an underground network of hyphae.) In the garden, gilled mushrooms commonly sprout from landscaping mulch. They even inhabit the arid desert. The desert shaggy mane (*Podaxis pistillaris*) fruits from dry washes after significant rainfall, emerging like a large, fibrous, and dirtied Q-tip.

Another reason to become acquainted with gilled mushrooms is the fact that the *Amanita* genus contains some of the most poisonous mushrooms. The most diabolical name belongs to a group of similar, all-white fungi known as destroying angels (*Amanita bisporigera, A. ocreata, A. virosa*). Donning a skirtlike ring around the stem, these mushrooms' elegance belies the presence of amatoxins that cause severe illness and death.

With nearly as rebellious a moniker, the death cap (*Amanita phalloides*) contains the same amatoxins and is responsible for 90 percent of mushroom-related fatalities worldwide. Unlike the odorless destroying angel, the death cap gives off an ammonia-tinged scent as they mature. (The smell has also been likened to honey or raw potatoes, a sign of the complex mixture of molecules the mushroom emits.)

Both the death cap and destroying angel can be mistaken for edible gilled mushrooms, making it imperative that you don't eat any wild mushroom without professional guidance or experience. But don't let their dangerous reputation stop you from admiring amanitas up close (or giving them a sniff). The mindful mushroom hunter appreciates all fungi for their peculiarities and presence, understanding their existence is independent of our own curiosity.

MINDFUL

ACTIVITY

Making a spore print with gilled mushrooms is easy! This works best with a mature, slightly moist mushroom. Remove the stem and place the cap, gills down, on a piece of paper. Cover with a cup or bowl and leave overnight. The next day, carefully lift the cup and cap to reveal a spore print.

OMPHALOTUS
OLIVASCENS

CRATERELLUS
FOETIDUS

CANTHARELLUS
CIBARIUS

TRUMPET-SHAPED MUSHROOMS

When searching for mushrooms, experts and amateurs alike generally rely upon their sense of sight. Yet with practice, you can discern the presence of certain mushrooms guided by your nose. The ripe stone fruit perfume emitted by black trumpets (*Craterellus foetidus*), the bouquet of apricots in the vicinity of chanterelles (*Cantharellus cibarius* and other species), and the strong, sweet smell of jack-o'-lanterns (*Omphalotus* species) are three odors that have evolved to appeal to the olfactory glands. Attracted by the smell, insects, mammals, and possibly humans then aid the mushrooms in spore dispersal.

These three mushrooms aren't just odiferous; they also fall under the category of trumpet-shaped mushrooms. Fruit bodies in this group resemble a trumpet, vase, or funnel. Peer under the cap, and you'll notice that some trumpet-shaped fungi, such as the oyster mushroom, exhibit true gills. Oyster mushrooms (*Pleurotus ostreatus*) also have an ammonia-tinged scent that imprints onto the memory. Other trumpet-shaped mushrooms, such as chanterelles, exhibit *false gills*: frilled ridges or folded membranes running from cap to stem.

Trumpet-shaped mushrooms often emerge under trees and from leaf litter, moss, or buried rotten wood. Chanterelles fruit under trees with which the fungi have mycorrhizal relationships, such as oak, pine, and spruce. A few days of steady rainfall in late summer, autumn, or occasionally winter is usually enough to arouse the mushrooms. Sunrise-yellow and orange fruit bodies make them easy to spot amid brown litterfall. If you find chanterelles once, take note. With the right conditions, they can often emerge in the same spot for years.

While chanterelles are prized wild edibles, there are some toxic look-alikes, notably jack-o'-lanterns. These pumpkin-hued mushrooms are often confused for chanterelles, but inspection reveals they have true gills rather than the chanterelle's veinlike, forked structure. Often found in clusters at the base of dead or dying trees (commonly oaks), these saprophytic mushrooms turn wood into nutrients for surrounding plants and animals. Jack-o'-lanterns are poisonous if eaten but are a favorite for their glowing personality. At night, they glow a dim but ominous pale green. This bioluminescence attracts insects, who spread the spores to other ailing or dead trees.

Not all the mushrooms in this category have a noticeable scent. However, after a consistent rain, many have a pronounced smell, mingling with the fragrance of petrichor and dampened organic matter. Learning how to find fungi by scent alone is a mushroom hunter's party trick, one worthy of tooting your own horn—or trumpet—about.

BOLETES

Ask a crayon-fisted child to draw a mushroom, and chances are they will outline something that looks strikingly like a bolete. Boletes are fleshy mushrooms of a cheerful, cherubic nature. They command attention with their often-thick stems (some with comically paunchy proportions), conspicuous colors, and spongy, hamburger-shaped caps.

Unlike a gilled mushroom, the inside of a bolete's cap is tightly packed with tiny, vertically oriented tubes. On the surface, these resemble pores. You may be tempted to press the underside of a bolete cap, especially with a larger specimen that can reach nearly 10 inches [25 cm] across. The texture is pleasingly similar to moistened memory foam.

If you're curious and have a pocketknife on hand, cut a bolete in half lengthwise. You'll be able to inspect a cross section of the tubes inside the cap. This is where the mushroom produces spores—nature's version of a miniature spore missile silo. As the bolete matures, they discharge the spores from the cap's perforated bottom to be carried off by the wind.

In an interesting twist, a bolete's cap and pores often differ in color. It's also not uncommon to find boletes with a stem as vibrant as American-cheese yellow topped with a sangria-hued cap, or vice versa. Some boletes can even change colors! For example, when bruised or cut, the cornflower bolete (*Gyroporus cyanescens*) immediately stains a dazzling blue. This transformation is caused by the presence of the oxygen-sensitive molecule *gyrocyanin*. Other boletes can stain brown, black, red, pink, or green.

The most well-known bolete, *Boletus edulis*, is a formidably sized fungus. Crowned with the common name of king bolete (and also known as cèpe, porcini, and penny bun), they're prized for culinary value. However, we strongly caution against foraging these if you aren't experienced with identification. This is mostly because some boletes are poisonous but also because boletes are notoriously infested by wiggly maggots. Older specimens may host an unappetizing party of fungus gnat, beetle, fly, and moth larvae gorging upon the flesh.

Boletes in the *Suillus* genus have slimy or sticky caps, earning them common names like sticky cap, sticky bun, and slippery Jack. Some believe the slime on the caps allows the mushrooms to withstand cold temperatures, acting as a sort of antifreeze. The slime is so viscous it can be difficult to remove from fingertips.

Summer and autumn are generally the best times to look for boletes. Most have mycorrhizal relationships with trees. Find one bolete, and you're likely to find several more nearby. So, if you're walking beneath hardwoods or conifers such as oak and pines, scan for bulges in the duff. A light swipe of a hiking pole or branch may reveal an emerging bolete you can poke, prod, and admire.

BOLETES

POLYPORES

W hen the spring rains have long since passed and summer has dried other fungi into a withered memory, polypore mushrooms continue to thrive. Some polypores fruit annually, but many of these fungi survive from year to year, withstanding both dry spells and frost. The secret to these (mostly saprobic) mushrooms' success is their tough, hard flesh and threadlike hyphae. Infiltrating wood, they subsist upon cellulose even when the days have gone dry.

Resilient survivors of the woods, polypores take their name from the Greek words *poly*, meaning several, and *poros*, meaning pore. Like boletes, they have numerous spore-bearing tubes on the underside of the cap. However, unlike their spongier counterparts, polypores tend to be woody, leathery, or corky and the tubes cannot be easily separated from the cap. In fact, the tubes are arranged so tightly, they can give the appearance of a completely smooth surface. A magnifying glass or macro lens reveals this totally tubular array upon close inspection.

Protruding from stumps, fallen logs, twigs, living trees, and the ground under conifers and hardwoods, polypores can grow singly or in great numbers. Growing with and without stems, they may have circular or semicircular caps or resemble shelves, fans, funnels, hooves, or even rosettes. Sometimes, a polypore fruiting body (often called a *bracket fungus*) growing on a tree trunk just right can look like a misshapen nose or ears. Polypores like the artist's conk (*Ganoderma applanatum*) can resemble plump pancakes, golden brown on top and lighter underneath. The lingzhi or reishi mushroom (*Ganoderma lingzhi*) glistens with a richly lacquered cap, while turkey tails (*Trametes versicolor*) can envelop the length of a dead or dying tree trunk, giving the appearance of scales. Others, like hen of the woods (*Grifola frondosa*) and chicken of the woods

(*Laetiporus* species) earned their nicknames from their ruffled-feather-like appearance.

The aforementioned artist's conk can grow steadily for more than a decade, radiating rings of earthen color like an abstract sunset. When discovered with its firm, velvety white underside intact, this mushroom invites artistic expression. A sharp object like a knife, stick, or even a fingernail can leave a permanent, brown-stained imprint, making *Ganoderma applanatum* a popular canvas for the artistically inclined.

Though polypores have recently gained popularity as health supplements, they've long been appreciated by many cultures. In *Puhpohwee for the People*, ethnobotanist Keewaydinoquay Pechel notes the Anishinabe peoples of the Great Lakes region have gathered polypores for medicine, fire starters, and ceremonial purposes. On the other side of the world, birch polypores were among the possessions of Ötzi, the five-thousand-year-old "Iceman" whose mummified body was found in the Alps. In China, lingzhi mushrooms have been revered as medicine for at least two thousand years. Beyond working with polypores, we can also simply enjoy spending time with them and appreciate their role in their ecosystems—breaking down wood and recycling nutrients back into the soil, air, and water.

MINDFUL

ACTIVITY

Mushrooms often rely on air currents to carry their spores and continue their life cycle. While mushroom hunting, turn your awareness to your breath as you inhale and exhale. Consider how your respiration connects you to mushrooms and all life on Earth.

CORDYCEPS (ON AN ANT)

XYLARIA POLYMORPHA

CLUB MUSHROOMS

I magine walking through the woods and stumbling upon a small, gnarled hand emerging from the ground. Congratulations, you're the fortunate witness of *Xylaria polymorpha,* a.k.a. dead-man's-fingers. This ghastly mushroom is renowned for frightening visitors of the forest.

Dead-man's-fingers are arguably the most heart-stopping example of club mushrooms, a group lacking gills, pores, or teeth. Club fungi appear in various elongated and roughly club-shaped fruit bodies. (Some more closely resemble spindles or fans.) While not all of them look as unsettling as *Xylaria polymorpha,* the group is filled with common names evoking appendages, including fairy fingers, dead man's toes, and our favorite, the hairy earthtongue.

Generally moisture loving, club mushrooms may be found growing singly or in groups upon well-rotted wood, damp soil, humus, moss, or grass, or in bogs and seeps. A great many are saprotrophic, breaking down and feeding on decaying organic matter. Some are mycorrhizal and rely upon subterranean partnerships with the roots of specific plants. Others are *lichenized*, having evolved relationships with algae.

And then there are the parasitic club mushrooms. If you've ever perused the supplements section of a pharmacy, you've probably seen the word *cordyceps* gracing a few labels. These, too, are club mushrooms. *Cordyceps* fungi have earned a bit of pop culture recognition, both for their reputed health benefits and their spine-chilling life cycle. Most *Cordyceps* species reproduce in a wondrously horrific fashion by infecting insects such as ants, caterpillars, and cicadas. The mycelium takes over the insect's body, and then the fungus fruits— often through the head of its host.

Less disturbing are the delicate *Clavaria fragilis* mushrooms. Known as fairy fingers, they emerge as slender spindles resembling white bean sprouts. Matchstick-like *Mitrula* mushrooms have white stems capped with yellow or orange. Common to boggy places with plenty of rotting vegetation, they are nicknamed swamp beacons or bog beacons. Their luminous colors are easily spotted against a murky environment.

Even though club mushrooms are mostly modest in size and often compared to matchsticks, worms, and other spindly forms, there are examples that live up to their category's namesake. The cudgel-shaped *Clavariadelphus pistillaris* and similarly formed *Clavariadelphus truncatus* grow to sizable proportions and inspire visions of a caveman's weapon. The former can grow especially large, up to nearly a foot [30 cm] tall. David Arora, author of *Mushrooms Demystified*, describes another large club fungus, *Clavariadelphus occidentalis*, as tasting reminiscent of stale rope. We'll take his word for it and advise you to do the same!

CORAL MUSHROOMS

Y ou might rub your eyes in disbelief the first time you spot a coral mushroom. These mushrooms are the spitting image of corals found on the ocean floor, but in miniature. Peer closely, and some reveal a disconcerting resemblance to gangly arms reaching toward the sky in silent praise. Some look like a collection of antlers; others like defoliated, gummy trees. They're often mesmerizing in their intricacy.

If one imagines the classic capped and gilled mushroom as the houses of the woodland, coral mushrooms are the trees and streetlamps. Like club mushrooms (page 73), coral mushrooms share the absence of a cap, gills, and pores. Shaped like branched corals or slender spindles, they can have rounded, pointed, forked, toothed, or crown-like tips.

In Tlaxcala, Mexico, coral mushrooms in the genus *Ramaria* are known as *escobetas*, named after the small scrubbing brushes used to clean pots.

Commonly buff to beige in color, coral mushrooms also exist in sulfur yellows, rusted oranges, riotous reds, punkish pinks, ashy grays, and angelic whites. Many change colors as they age, making them tricky to identify. The more flamboyant examples of *Ramaria* fruit in colors reminiscent of grape bubble gum or even macaroni and cheese. And it would be near impossible to miss the bright orange-red spindles of flame fungus (*Clavulinopsis sulcata*) against a backdrop of drab plant litter. Squint and they can look like tiny campfire flames drawn by a child.

Though genetically unrelated to the branched and spindle varieties, the genus *Sparassis* also gets lumped into the coral category. Often found at the base of dead or dying conifers, *Sparassis* mushrooms have cream-colored lobes reminiscent of brain corals found in ocean reefs. Wavy and rosette-like, they might also inspire a desire to cook egg noodles or cauliflower for dinner.

Sparassis are mildly parasitic, but most coral mushrooms are mycorrhizal or saprobic. Many grow on the ground or on mossy soil under trees. However, it's not unusual to pick up a coral mushroom to discover they are attached to a twig, leaves, or even a pine cone (making them extremely photogenic). The white- or buff-colored crown-tipped coral fungus (*Artomyces pyxidatus*) often appears to be growing from soil. But dig around and underneath, and you'll almost always find a piece of rotting wood from which the decomposer is feeding. This reminds us that much of what we consider a fungus is only a fruiting expression of a life below the surface.

HYDNUM REPANDUM

HYDNELLUM PECKII

TOOTHED MUSHROOMS

Mushroom hunting generally rewards a "head down" approach: scanning for a suggestive bump emerging from the fallen leaves or getting on hands and knees to inspect the undersides of fallen logs. Toothed mushrooms often require an entirely different strategy. These mushrooms frequently grow up on tree trunks or hang from branches instead of emerging from soil.

Fungi with teeth (or spines) produce some of the most arresting fruit bodies you'll ever find. Some, like the bleeding tooth fungus, are just downright weird (more about this mushroom later). You certainly won't miss a lion's mane or bear's head tooth mushroom out in the wild, or even at your local farmer's market where they're commonly sold—they have striking pure white to off-white coloration, expressive shapes, and sometimes impressive girth.

Growing with or without stems and in clusters or in a solitary fluffy mass, these cloudlike mushrooms take forms open to imaginative interpretation. When encountering a bear's head tooth (*Hericium americanum*), one person may see an angelic pom-pom; another, a frozen patch of icicles. Other toothed mushrooms look convincingly like a head of cauliflower.

The most well-known toothed mushroom is the lion's mane (*Hericium erinaceus*). This shaggy-looking fungus sometimes grows to such considerable proportions (up to 4 feet [1.2 m] in diameter), it's not unreasonable to believe you've run into a white-haired sheepdog peering from behind a tree. In Japan, this mushroom is known as yamabushitake, or "those who sleep in the mountains."

From lions and bears to monkeys and satyrs, the common names of many toothed mushrooms evoke creatures of the forest.

Another highly sought-after fungus is the hedgehog mushroom (*Hydnum repandum*). Hedgehogs sport a more archetypal cap and stem, but in lieu of gills or pores, their undersides are carpeted in densely packed, fleshy "teeth."

Like hedgehog mushrooms, the bleeding tooth fungus (*Hydnellum peckii*) emerges from the ground. They are one of the more disturbing yet alluring mushrooms one may hope to find. This mushroom emerges rather unremarkably as a small, white, nondescript mass in a bed of fallen pine needles or near moss. Yet when the right moist conditions appear, the mushroom begins to sweat droplets of "blood" atop the cap. The liquid is actually just water absorbed from the ground and tinted by the fungus through osmosis. Mostly found in old-growth forests, *Hydnellum peckii* also goes by the more appealing nickname of strawberries and cream mushroom.

So, next time you find yourself in the woods, be sure to glance both up and down, and look out for various kinds of toothily grinning, flamboyantly tufted, and bloody messes of fruit bodies growing from trunks, stumps, and the ground or hanging from branches overhead.

MINDFUL

ACTIVITY

When you meet a mushroom—
whether they are growing at your feet
or up in a tree—get to know them
from multiple angles. Crouch down,
raise your eyes, tilt your head, look
under the cap. What do you notice
when you change your perspective?

CALVATIA GIGANTEA

LYCOPERDON
ECHINATUM

CALVATIA
SCULPTA

PUFFBALLS

Mushrooms are often inconspicuous, blending in among fallen leaves or peeking timidly from underneath rotting logs. Many are so small and so well camouflaged, spotting them requires considerable effort to "stop and stare" before our senses register their existence. Then there is the giant puffball (*Calvatia gigantea*). By all appearances, the giant puffball *wants* to be discovered.

An encounter with a giant puffball often begins with a case of mistaken identity. Standing out from the grass, the white spherical mass may initially appear to be a misplaced softball or even a volleyball. Only when you get nearer can you discern the almost perfectly white "ball" is something else entirely. The giant puffball is renowned for its ability to grow cartoonishly large. The largest puffball mushroom ever, as documented by Guinness World Records, was found in Slaithwaite, West Yorkshire, UK—a 66.5-inch (169 cm) whopper so large it required two sets of hands to securely cradle.

Without any discernible cap, stem, or hymenophore, puffballs are a bit of an oddity within the already weird world of mushrooms. While the giant puffball is rather conspicuous, other species are smaller and golf-ball-like or shaped more like a pear or pestle. Their surfaces may be smooth, spiked, or warty and range in color from brown to gray, white, and yellow. The spiny puffball (*Lycoperdon echinatum*) resembles a chestnut or tiny hedgehog, while the sculpted puffball (*Calvatia sculpta*) seems to be covered in peaks of meringue. All of these wonders are saprobic, helping to break down organic matter in their habitats. You may find them growing in grassy areas, soil, decaying wood, and places where the spores landed after hitchhiking on our feet—from parks to golf courses and along trail edges.

Puffballs (as well as earthstars, stinkhorns, and bird's-nest fungi) were once placed in a subgroup of fungi called *gasteroids* or *Gastero-mycetes*, which literally means "stomach fungi" in ancient Greek and Latin. These fungi have a stomach-like sac that contains the spores. Over time, the spore sac dehydrates into a powdery mass, discoloring and darkening to brown, yellow, or even purple.

When fully matured, all it takes is a firm push, poke, or prod (a stick makes a great tool for this purpose), and the puffball plumes a cloud of spores numbering in the billions or even trillions. Don't be shy stepping on or even punting a puffball, either. You're simply helping disperse the spores and guaranteeing another generation of puffballs; your footsteps afterward will be laden with spores to be spread far and wide!

NOTE: *Humans and dogs should avoid directly inhaling large amounts of puffball spores, which can cause lycoperdonosis, a rare respiratory illness.*

EARTHSTARS

When searching for the stars, our eyes naturally gravitate toward the heavens. For mushroom hunters, a downward glance across pastures or under trees can reveal a different sort of constellation.

Earthstars emerge from the soil with nondescript, closed, rounded fruit bodies that may resemble a tawny mushroom cap, a small, filthy onion, or an acorn past its prime. Inside lies a spongy mass. In time, this dries into a powder keg of spores ready to be dispersed by a well-placed raindrop or animal's footstep. But before they can release their spores, the mushroom must unfurl their leathery outer layer, forming the semblance of a star with pointed rays. (Imagine peeling back the skin of a stout, round banana.)

Some earthstars lie flat against the ground, while others have rays that arch back, lifting the spore sac upward. *Myriostoma coliforme*'s spore case is perforated with many small holes, inspiring common names like *pepper pot* and *saltshaker*. (As with puffballs, be careful not to directly inhale large amounts of spores; see page 89.)

Hygroscopic, or barometer, earthstars in the *Astraeus* genus rely on humidity to pull back their pointed rays. Differing rates of moisture absorption across parts of the rays activate the unfolding mechanism. In dry weather, the rays close back up.

Debate rages on whether certain earthstars are mycorrhizal or saprobic, but they are typically found growing under trees, across pastures, and along woodland edges, roadsides, and other disturbed areas. Their generally earthy coloration camouflages well against soil or leaf litter. Easily overlooked, they are most often found closed or after their fruit bodies have exhausted their spores. But when discovered in an open state, earthstar mushrooms offer a wondrous sight.

The taxonomy of earthstars is rife with examples of *convergent evolution* (instances when similar features evolve independently). Fungi in the genus *Geastrum* are considered "true" earthstars. *Astraeus* mushrooms may share a starlike appearance, but recent research points toward a closer relation to boletes. And even more bewildering, *Geastrum* earthstars are kin to stinkhorns and coral mushrooms despite their disparate appearances. *Astraeus* are mycorrhizal with a range of plants, while *Myriostoma* are saprobic, and scientists aren't sure about *Geastrum*.

Regardless of which kind you happen upon, if you find one at the right time, when the spore sac is ready to give up the ghost, try gently poking with a stick. The slightest pressure will coerce delightful puffs of spores from their small, puckered orifices. Do this too many times and you will be left with the shriveled remains of a dead star that has fulfilled their purpose: giving life to new galaxies of earthstars elsewhere.

NIDULA
NIVEOTOMENTOSA

CRUCIBULUM
LAEVE

BIRD'S-NEST MUSHROOMS

Easily overlooked, bird's-nest mushrooms compel us to change our perspective. They're Lilliputian, measuring mere millimeters, and commonly grow concealed among mulch, leaf litter, or decaying wood. (They can also be found growing from the dung of herbivores, but we won't blame you if you pass on the opportunity to inspect that particular medium closely.) You've probably unknowingly passed by communities of these tiny mushrooms numerous times. But after training the senses about when and where to look, an observant mushroom hunter can regularly find this fungus on trails or around the yard.

In fact, if you're a gardener, a community of these saprobic mushrooms may be in your garden beds or wood chip mulch at this very moment, either actively growing or silently biding their time. (We find tiny fungus nests filled with pearlescent black "eggs" growing en masse every year from the soil in our vegetable planter box.) The spores ride along inconspicuously with nutrient-rich organic matter, only for tens or even hundreds to suddenly germinate when adequate dampness, warmth, and shade provide favorable conditions for the mycelium to fruit.

Initially, they appear as little cups or urns covered with a thin membrane known as the *epiphragm*—like miniature crème brûlée—but they eventually open, exposing a collection of lentil-shaped eggs in groups averaging three to six per nest. Colors of bird's-nest eggs range from white to yellow, brown, tan, or gray.

The adorableness of bird's-nest mushrooms makes them must-see fungi for the mushroom curious. But wait, there's more to admire! Each of those eggs is actually a thick-walled delivery mechanism encasing millions of spores. Bird's-nest fungi evolved the cup-shaped nests so that when a water droplet lands just so, the force ejects one or numerous eggs with surprising impact from the nest, scattering spores upward of 6 feet [180 cm]. If you want to see this in action, use a water dropper to splash some water directly from above into the cup. If you're lucky, you might witness an egg "fly" the nest!

Depending on the species, each egg sac is either covered in gel or connected to a thread-like coiled *funicular cord* with a sticky end that unfurls as it's shot out from the nest (this is the mushroom realm's version of a bungee cord). The cord or gel is tenaciously adhesive, sticking the egg onto blades of grass, twigs, plant stalks, or anything nearby. The egg then dries out and eventually splits open, releasing millions of spores to ride the wind far and wide and begin the cycle anew.

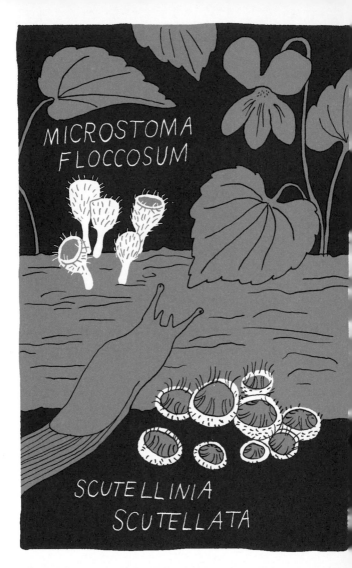

MICROSTOMA
FLOCCOSUM

SCUTELLINIA
SCUTELLATA

CUP MUSHROOMS

I f you're walking in the woods and spot what appears at first glance to be bright red drops of spilled paint, cast-off orange peels, or little cups resembling a fairy's tablescape, you might be in the presence of cup mushrooms. These fungi all share a characteristic concave shape. But while "cup" is a general description, they do vary: some are deep like a bowl or urn, others shallow like a flattened saucer, and yet others look like tiny goblets inviting a toast. Mushrooms in this group may or may not have a stem. (For cups with eggs inside, see bird's-nest mushrooms, page 95.)

Some larger species of cup mushrooms can be found with a diameter of up to 8 inches [20 cm] and exhibit wavy edges with a less distinctly cup-shaped cap. However, most cup mushrooms are small, measuring only around 0.2 inches [0.5 cm]. Thankfully, they often fruit in dense clusters, freckling whatever substrate they're found upon and making them easier to spot. (Always peek around the shaded corners of fallen logs.)

Along with being small, many cup mushrooms camouflage into the background organic matter, muted and inconspicuous. But others fruit flamboyantly and are easily discernible from a distance despite their modest size. The eyelash cup (*Scutellinia scutellata*) is one of the more fanciful examples: small, red cups embellished with fringes of tiny hairs, provoking thoughts of mascara and a wink. The orange peel fungus (*Aleuria aurantia*) and its less common counterpart, the moldy orange peel fungus (*Caloscypha fulgens*), are both often mistaken for the remains of a hiker's snack. The yellow fairy cup (*Bisporella citrina*), which rarely exceeds about 0.1 inches [3 mm] in diameter, is as bright as scrambled eggs and easy to find against sodden dark logs.

Cup mushrooms generally require sufficient moisture and a nutritious substrate to feed upon. Soil, fallen leaves, and wood, such as fallen twigs or rotting branches, will all suffice for these decomposers. (Cup fungi are generally considered to be saprobic; however, studies suggest some may have mycorrhizal relationships with trees.) They also occasionally fruit from herbivore dung, offering a possible incentive to investigate patties or pellets.

The cups themselves operate as the spore-producing structures of the fungi. As they rely upon the impact of a well-aimed raindrop to launch their spores into the world, these fungi are the mycological embodiment of "my cup runneth over."

PHALLUS INDUSIATUS

PHALLUS IMPUDICUS

ASEROE RUBRA

STINKHORNS

The name speaks for itself: a mushroom so foul smelling, you're more likely to notice them by nose before spotting them by eye. The fetid bouquet of a stinkhorn mushroom is often compared to a rotting carcass floating in an outhouse. And these mushrooms don't just smell awful—they fruit in a menagerie of shapes that can plant doubt about whether their origins are truly earthly in nature.

The mature stinkhorn's odor is attributed to *volatile organic compounds* (chemicals that easily become vapor) such as oligosulfides, hexadecane, pentadecane, nonadecane, and dimethyl trisulfides. This cocktail of twenty-two compounds happens to smell just like necrotic lesions (or so we're told). What's more, the mushroom's spore-bearing mass is coated in a glistening mucus in hues of stool green, fecal brown, or deathly black.

As horrific as this all seems, stinkhorns' odor and strange morphology attract the frenzied buzz of carrioneating insects like flies and beetles. What is nauseating to our senses they find an irresistible treat. After supping on the gooey secretions, the visiting insects depart with spores clinging to their legs or in their digestive tracts, to be relocated through their droppings.

Initially emerging from an egg-like structure, stinkhorns mature into a phallic, column, claw, lattice, or cage-like shape. Certain stinkhorns in the genus *Phallus* have earned nicknames like deadman's cock and prick mushroom, thanks to their form. Prodigious growers, stinkhorns have been measured to grow up to 4 to 6 inches [10 to 15 cm] per hour, and with enough force to fracture asphalt!

This is not to say stinkhorns do not have their admirable qualities. They are in fact some of the most visually wondrous fungi you'll ever find. Varieties such as the bridal veil (*Phallus indusiatus*) don a lacy, white "skirt" that any fashionista would admire. As the veil falls to the ground, it offers terrestrial insects a ladder to reach the spores.

The scarlet tendrils of the octopus stinkhorn (*Clathrus archeri*) are a bit more sinister looking but subjectively more awesome than awful. And then there is the anemone stinkhorn (*Aseroe rubra*) common to the Hawaiian Islands, Australia, New Zealand, and parts of southeastern North America. This mushroom's "claws" seem to be grasping from a thick central stem, giving the appearance of a torrid sea creature having their worst day ever.

Stinkhorns are surprisingly common across the world, often growing on well-watered lawns or sprouting from moist garden mulch. The fruiting bodies of these saprobic fungi are fairly short lived. After "blooming" for only a few hours during or after wet weather, they decompose into a putrid goo. The experience of finding one is likely to be remembered through the senses of sight and smell in equal measure.

CLATHUS RUBER

MINDFUL

ACTIVITY

What we call a stinkhorn might be the sweet food of life to other animals. Our interpretations of our senses are subjective, attuned to our own preferences. Is it possible to be present to the smell without immediately categorizing it as "good" or "bad"?

XYLOBOLUS FRUSTULATUS

CRUST MUSHROOMS

F aced with a name like crust mushroom, you could be excused for harboring low expectations. Whether it be on pizza or fungus, the crust is often dismissed as inessential. But despite their humble appearance, these mushrooms are anything but superfluous. Crust mushrooms encompass an array of highly adaptable fungi that play essential ecological roles and deserve our appreciation.

Without a well-defined shape nor gills, pores, or teeth, their "wow" factor admittedly rates low compared to other fungi. Many crust mushrooms are drab and inconspicuous to anyone but the most inquisitive mushroom hunter willing to literally turn over every log. They often grow in patches or sheets of discoloration against the surface of wood, like an affliction you might want to have a doctor check. Most are saprobic, subsisting on the dead wood they fruit from. Some species are parasitic on living wood or possibly mycorrhizal with trees.

Crust mushrooms' spore-bearing surfaces may appear smooth, wrinkled, cracked, flattened, bumpy, warty, or simply crusty, and these mushrooms are easily overlooked against the backdrop of their substrate. Take, for example, the ceramic parchment fungus (*Xylobolus frustulatus*), which has a proclivity for covering rotting hardwood in polygonal patterns. Most people would hardly give it a glance. But peer closer and the tiled fruit bodies look almost like a form of mycological code waiting to be decrypted.

Of all mushrooms, crust fungi can be a test and indicator of a mushroom hunter's observational skills and passion for finding fungi. Crusts tend to be tough and can often be found year-round on dead wood, even when other mushrooms aren't fruiting. They're often unnoticed due to their relatively small and almost two-dimensional growth. Yet some crust mushrooms are rather eye-catching, such as the cobalt crust (*Terana coerulea*), which fruits in an intense dark blue worthy of a van Gogh palette.

Mushrooms in the *Stereum* genus may look like polypores from above. However, careful observation reveals they don't have pores. Finding some offers an opportune moment to bring out a small hand lens or a macro lens for your camera or smartphone. False turkey tails (*Stereum ostrea*, *S. hirsutum*, *S. complicatum*) look like little leathery fans or brackets with concentric bands of color—buff, orange, yellow, brown. These crust mushrooms resemble their coveted counterparts, turkey tails (page 68), except instead of pores, they exhibit a completely smooth underside. Becoming aware of such subtle differences is what separates the casual observer from the astute enthusiast.

JELLY MUSHROOMS

I f you're someone who has often been told to "look, but don't touch," then jelly mushrooms are sure to become a favorite. Because if there are any fungi a mycophile *should* touch, these semitranslucent mushrooms fit the bill. With their rubbery or gelatinous fruit bodies, jellies defy expectations of what a mushroom should look and feel like.

One often encounters (and overlooks) jelly mushrooms in their dormant, desiccated state during warmer months. You might mistake them for a discarded piece of chewing gum, a withered leaf, or even an unappetizing prune stuck into the seams of an old log. Fruiting from wood or tree litter, these mushrooms bide their time during dry seasons while waiting for rain or snowmelt. When enough water has soaked into their flexible cell walls, the dehydrated fruit bodies swell with succulence. Typically found in cool, shady spots, jelly fungi can be decomposers of wood and humus, as well as parasitic on other fungi and lichens.

Some expand into clusters that resemble brains with irregular lobed folds. Others take shape as minuscule splatters dotting hardwoods or ruffles reminiscent of a nylon shower puff. A few develop into viscous pustules daring only the most adventurous to touch. One of the most curious examples is the cat's tongue (*Pseudohydnum gelatinosum*), which takes on the ghostly, translucent white silhouette of a toothed mushroom, an apparition of the forest. Fungi in the genus *Auricularia*, commonly known as wood ear mushrooms, often grow gregariously across spans of dead or weakened wood. Resembling a lineup of rubbery brown human ears, they seem to be listening on behalf of the forest.

Many jelly mushrooms are colorful, especially when young and fully hydrated. The golden jelly or witches'-butter (*Tremella mesenterica*) has a rich yellow appearance. Even when small or solitary, this mushroom is easily spotted from afar, so vibrant is their coloration (which is further enhanced by their proclivity to grow from darkened, water-soaked logs). Occasionally you'll find *Tremella* mushrooms growing in prolific linear clumps across a branch, like the outstretched arm of a flamboyantly ruffled shirt. The apricot jelly (*Guepinia helvelloides*) is another colorful example, a charming fungus with a trumpet or curled tongue shape tinted orange to salmon pink.

When young, crystal brain mushrooms (*Myxarium nucleatum*) take on a slimy translucency. In shaded light, they look like globs of liquid mercury and are an example of a jelly fungus you're more likely to investigate with the aid of a stick or hiking pole rather than the tip of a finger (and understandably so).

Jelly mushrooms can be especially interesting to observe as they transform in texture and translucency. Whenever you can, revisit them over a period of hours, days, weeks, or even months. What changes do you notice in size, shape, color, or even odor?

MORELS, TRUE AND FALSE

Morels' reputation as a culinary delicacy makes them some of the most highly sought-after mushrooms. But the popularity of the *Morchella* genus is not just about their prized taste. A large part of their appeal stems from *when* these wrinkled wonders appear. Emerging at the beginning of spring, just as tree buds rouse from their winter slumber, morels offer many communities one of the year's first outdoor activities. In other words, the joy of finding them is about the journey as much as the destination. (Morels may also be found in summer in some colder areas, or occasionally in autumn and winter.)

Growing near hardwoods and conifers, as well as on mulch and alkaline soil, morels can have mycorrhizal or saprobic relationships with particular trees, like apple, pine, ash, aspen, elm, oak, and sycamore. The network of mycelium stirs into action with a disturbance to the soil—most notably wildfires, but also excavations, grazing animals, or activity along the edges of woodland paths. These stressors set off a mycorrhizal response, resulting in the growth of fruit bodies.

Morels may represent springtime renewal, but they can also be somewhat fickle, showing up abundantly one year, then disappearing without a trace. Even experienced mushroom foragers can come back empty handed. If you're fond of *Where's Waldo?* or "spot the difference" puzzles, searching for morels can deliver similar gratification, rewarding perseverance and perception. (Or occasionally dumb luck, as is often the case when people find morels growing beneath park benches or from garden mulch.)

Morels lack gills or pores and their caps have more or less vertical ridges and pits. Some compare the wrinkled folds to honeycomb. Their flesh is thin and brittle, breaking to reveal a hollow interior spanning from cap to stem, which are fused together. Often categorized as "blacks" and "yellows," morels camouflage well against the ground. But once you find one, it becomes easier and easier to spot them in numbers, making for a rewarding treasure hunt.

Morels do have a few doppelgängers, but these look-alikes are not too difficult to discern. False morels in the *Gyromitra* and *Verpa* genera have thimble-, brain-, or cup-shaped caps that are more wrinkled, lobed, or folded than the true morel's ridges and pits. *Gyromitra* are not hollow but rather have cottony tissue or chambers inside. *Verpa* are hollow inside, but their caps are "free hanging" meaning they're only attached at the very top of the stem. Mushrooms in the *Helvella* genus lack ridges and are shaped like cups or saddles, inspiring their common name of elfin saddles.

Of course, as a mindful mushroom hunter, finding a "true" or "false" morel can be equally fascinating. Every mushroom gifts us an opportunity to hone our sense of awareness.

They WEAVE A WEB of reciprocity, of giving and taking. In this way, the trees all ACT AS ONE because the fungi have CONNECTED them. Through unity, survival. All FLOURISHING IS MUTUAL. Soil, fungus, tree, squirrel, boy—all are the beneficiaries of RECIPROCITY.

—Robin Wall Kimmerer, *Braiding Sweetgrass*

V.

INTERCONNECTEDNESS

The hope of finding a chanterelle or puffball may inspire our hunt, but in time, we awaken to more than mushrooms. As we spend time outside, our senses can ground us in the present moment and the wonders all around us—from pill bugs to trees, the sensation of air currents on our skin, and the scent of soil after a rain. Paying attention to temperature and humidity, sight, sound, smell, taste, and texture, we become aware of not just the rhythms of the seasons but also the subtleties of a particular bend in the trail or a microclimate in our backyard. We tune into a fuller story of the Earth and the teachings offered to us.

We also find that, like us, no mushroom is alone. These aboveground marvels are beacons alerting us to an intricate network of the microscopic and unseen. Fungi are the connective tissue, their mycelia keeping soil healthy and fostering relationships among plants, animals, fungi, and microbes. Their roles as industrious decomposers teach us about the cycles of life, death, and continuation.

Every time we hunt for mushrooms, whether it's in a local park, during a camping trip or on our daily walk to work, we have an opportunity to be mindful. To exercise curiosity, developing a deeper awareness of our surroundings, suspending judgment, and becoming comfortable with change. Mindfulness practices have been shown to have meaningful benefits, such as reduced stress, anxiety, and chronic pain. But this isn't merely about individual self-optimization.

Rather, it's about recognizing how we are interdependent participants in the world. When we let go of our inward focus, mindfulness also offers benefits to our communities. Through the connections we notice, we find that we are not separate from our environment. How might this practice of interacting with other species affect how we live on Earth?

Perhaps our culture's growing interest in mushrooms stems from seeing parallels between their mycelial networks and our own internet-connected lives. But more than that, perhaps we sense that we can learn alongside them about the possibilities of building relationships that foster reciprocity, resilience, and collective flourishing. In return, we can be a force for ensuring that fungi are appreciated and protected to do their essential work.

As you continue along your mushroom journey, we encourage you to share your enthusiasm and experience. Invite friends or family members on a mushroom hunt. Spread the joy and plant the spores of interest! Grow your community and connect with folks who are interested in not just mushrooms but also related spheres like habitat protection, gardening, wildlife conservancy, community science, foodways, herbal medicine, and more.

For our planet to thrive, it is vital that we become fluent in the language of the land. We must be aware of the intricate interdependencies unfolding all around us, whether perceptible or concealed from us. The mycorrhizal networks of mushrooms inscribe an ancient and enduring message into soil and wood in the mother tongue of the world. Their story is available to our senses if only we stop to pay attention.

Axford, Steve. "Fungi." The SmugMug site of Steve Axford. Accessed August 30, 2022. https://steveaxford.smugmug.com/Fungi/

Bierend, Doug. *In Search of Mycotopia: Citizen Science, Fungi Fanatics, and the Untapped Potential of Mushrooms.* White River Junction: Chelsea Green Publishing, 2021.

iNaturalist. Accessed August 30, 2022. https://www.inaturalist.org

Kimmerer, Robin Wall. *Braiding Sweetgrass: Indigenous Wisdom, Scientific Knowledge and the Teachings of Plants.* Minneapolis: Milkweed Editions, 2015.

Kuo, Michael. MushroomExpert.com. Accessed August 30, 2022. http://www.mushroomexpert.com

McCoy, Peter. *Radical Mycology: A Treatise on Seeing & Working With Fungi.* Portland, Oregon: Chthaeus Press, 2016.

Nhất Hạnh, Thích. *The Miracle of Mindfulness: An Introduction to the Practice of Meditation.* Boston: Beacon Press, 1976.

Pouliot, Alison. *The Allure of Fungi.* Clayton South: CSIRO Publishing, 2018.

Sheldrake, Merlin. *Entangled Life: How Fungi Make Our Worlds, Change Our Minds & Shape Our Futures.* New York: Random House, 2020.